MW01620598

Horst Schulz

Patchwork Knitting

Pullovers • Jackets • Waistcoats

Horst Schulz

Patchwork Knitting

Pullovers • Jackets • Waistcoats

Exciting new patchwork technique
Colourful, easy-to-knit patterns

Saprotex International

Contents

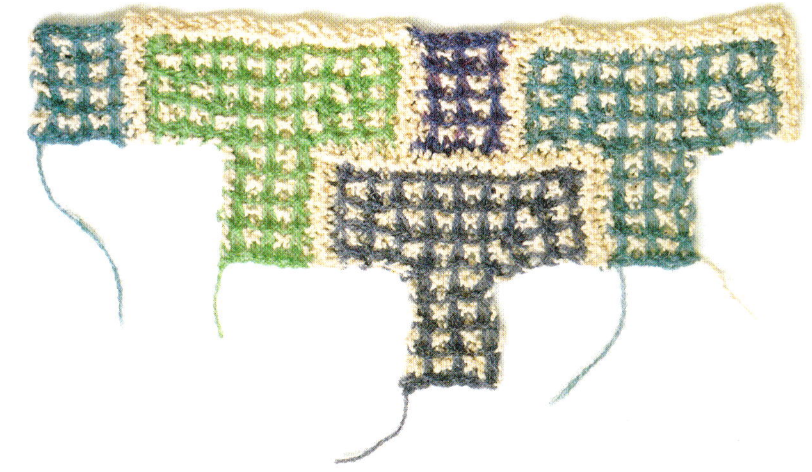

Introduction

'Patchwork Knitting' simply means thinking differently – forget the old idea that you can only knit horizontally. Knitting vertically, that is to say, in multicoloured narrow strips or using a patchwork technique, opens up new ways for those who are happy to experiment.

The idea of looking at knitting from a different perspective came to me long after I had learned to knit. At the time I was in charge of the customer advice sessions in the knitting department of a chain of shops for ladies' clothing. Over the years I encountered every kind of knitting problem imaginable. The most common problem always cropped up when knitting with many different colours – the complicated process of changing colours and untangling several balls of yarn severely tried my patience.

However, the problem also fascinated me. Taking the concept of patchwork blankets, which are made up of many different sections, I hit upon a new knitting technique. Why couldn't I also knit and join separate sections in different colours? This would solve the problem of the balls of yarn becoming entangled while at the same time making it possible to produce a gloriously colourful piece of knitting!

This simple idea has become the starting point of an endless variety of possibilities. I would like to introduce you to some of them in this book. Best of all, the 'patchwork knitting' technique will make you want to create your own combinations.

The principles on which 'patchwork knitting' is based are simple to understand. You can have fun knitting in an assortment of different colours without the bother of having to untangle many balls of yarn.

I hope you derive as much pleasure as I have discovering the endless possibilities that 'patchwork knitting' offers you.

The principles of 'patchwork knitting'

The principles of 'patchwork knitting' are quite simple: instead of painstakingly using different colours in one row, the colours are knitted vertically in strips or different shaped patches which are then joined into strips. The second strip in a different colour is attached to the first strip. In this way you only have to deal with one colour at a time. The strip technique also has the advantage that you can easily regulate the width of the work: it is not just the number of originally cast-on stitches that determine the final size, but also the number of strips.

With the help of a paper pattern you can achieve the desired size and shape without having the bother of undoing any stitches. As the separate coloured pieces are knitted individually, it is also quick and easy to correct the colours. If you have made a mistake in the colour, simply take the corresponding piece out and re-knit.

Finally, all the finished pullovers and jackets can be easily altered to fit a figure which has changed: if you have put on weight, simply join another strip to the garment. After a diet, take out a strip.

Assuming you already have some experience in knitting and know how to knit plain and purl and can cast on and off, the technique of 'patchwork knitting' is based on these simple principles.

The Essentials: The Edge Stitches

Correct edge stitches on both sides of the strips are imperative. This is the only way you can achieve neat joins between the individual strips and pieces. When making an edge stitch, the first stitch of each row is always worked knitwise into the back of the stitch (so that the thread is behind the needle), and the last stitch is slipped purlwise.

On each side of the strip a row of V-shaped edge stitches is produced, of which one edge stitch covers two rows. That is to say, 2 rows = 1 edge stitch.

When changing colours, make sure that the next thread is always taken up behind the previous one. Do not forget to weave the ends of the threads in immediately if possible.
Attention: weaving the ends of threads in does not work with rows of slip stitches! You can only do this in the next row of stitches.

My tip:

If edge stitches appear very loose you can simply tighten the yarn after knitting the second stitch.

1

2

Casting on new stitches

At the beginning of a new piece of work you can cast on the stitches using the needle and thumb method. However, at further stages of 'patchwork knitting' it is better to use the French (two needle) casting-on method as sometimes there is only one thread available for casting on stitches.

With the two needle method you can start knitting while casting on the stitches. As the illustrations show, a new stitch is cast on from the first stitch. You simply slip this new stitch onto the left needle and cast on the next stitch from it. This technique is preferable when further stitches are needed for a new square. In this way, casting on counts as the first row.

1 Cast on a new stitch from the first stitch of a row.
2 Slip the new stitch onto the left needle.
3 Now cast on the next stitch from the new stitch.
4 In this way you can cast on as many stitches as you like.

3

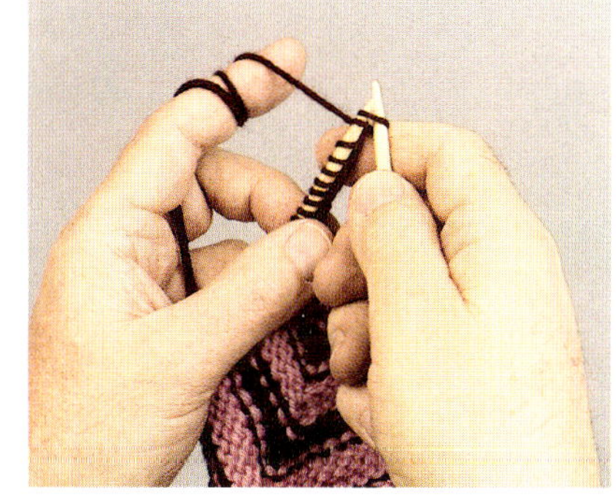

4

Knitting strips together

There are two methods of knitting the strips together. According to the method chosen, you can see the two adjoining rows of stitches either on the front or the reverse side.

Method 1: see diagram 1
Joining strip B to strip A knitwise

1. On strip B, slip the last stitch knitwise.
2. Pick up and knit a corresponding stitch from the side of strip A.
3. Pass slip stitch over this stitch.
4. Turn work and with yarn in front, slip the 1st stitch purlwise. Purl across row.
5. The result will be two rows of parallel stitches.

Method 2: see diagram 2
Joining strip B to strip A purlwise

1. On strip B slip the last stitch purlwise.
2. Pick up and purl corresponding stitch from the side of strip A.
3. Slip last 2 stitches onto left hand needle and purl these 2 stitches together.
4. Turn work and slip 1st stitch knitwise. Knit across row.

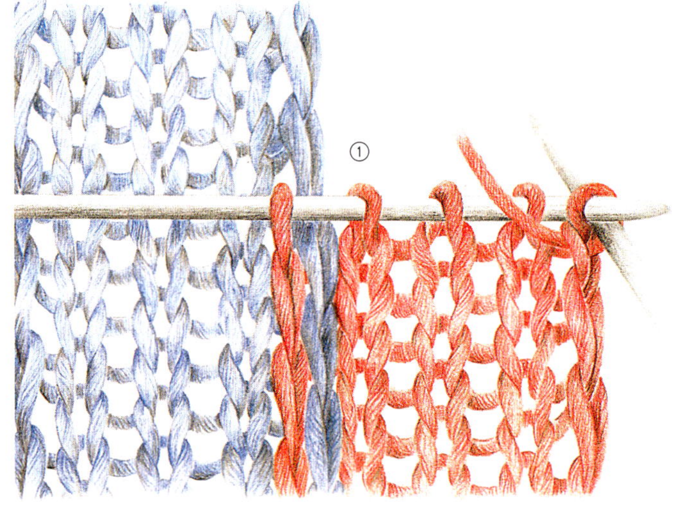

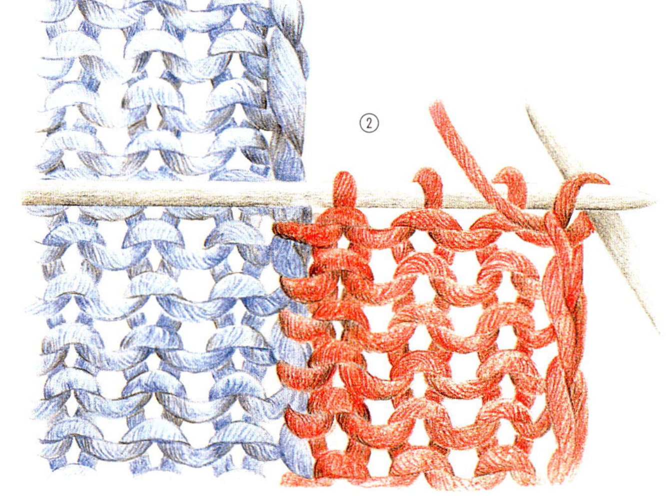

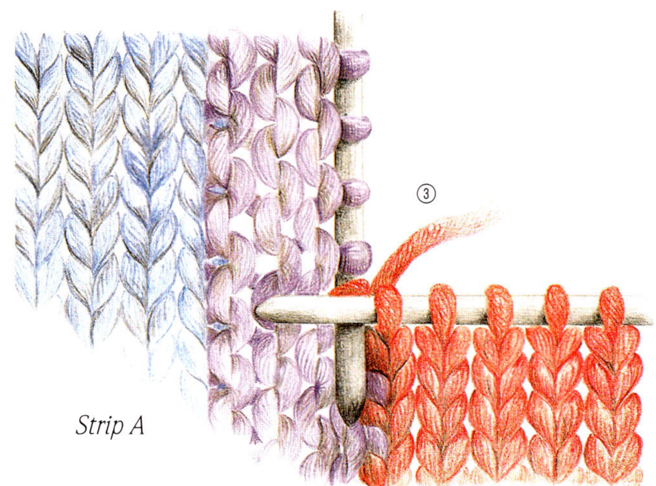

My tip:

Dark colours make it difficult to be able to recognise the edge stitches easily. Using a light background, a white tablecloth or a piece of paper can be very useful.

Method 3: see diagram 3

For many patterns I recommend you knit the strips together with a circular needle. To do so first pick up and knit new stitches on a circular needle from all the right-hand edge stitches of the finished strip=strip A. Now you do not have to spend a long time searching for the edge stitches, as you already have them on your needle. Of course, you can start knitting a few rows up and down with these stitches. Then cast on strip B with the right needle of a circular needle, and take the yarn in front of the knitting. Now again, as before, purl together the left edge stitch of strip B and the first stitch on the circular needle. On the reverse row take the yarn behind the knitting and slip the first stitch knitwise.

The photographs above show how the ends of the yarn are woven in when knitting stocking stitch. The working yarn is dark red. The pink yarn is woven in.

Weaving in the ends of the yarn

This method saves you having to sew the ends in later. You can weave in one to three ends of yarn for 7-10 cm on the reverse side. However, this is only possible when knitting stocking stitch. To do this, hold the ends of the yarn by the thumb and middle finger of the left hand. Now insert the needle into the stitch on the front side, place the yarn over the needle, and knit the stitch with the working yarn. Then for the next stitch the ends of the yarn remain under the needle. With this method – one up, one down – you can also take yarns in the second stitch upwards after the right-hand edge stitch.

The photographs on this page show how the yarns are woven in for rows of plain or purl. For moss stitch it is possible to weave in on both sides.

The ends of the yarn can also be woven in when knitting purl, as these pictures show. Again the working yarn is dark red, and the yarn being woven in is pink.

Materials

Here the colours of a particularly interesting pattern on bathroom wallpaper inspired the idea for the combination of yarns

Not only is the method of knitting different, you also need a different approach when buying your yarns.

You can choose to your heart's content from the assortment of colours and textures of the yarns on offer. The days are gone when you only considered buying yarns of the same type and batch number, because for 'patchwork knitting' many colours and many different shades are needed.

Use pictures, postcards, photographs, fabrics and wallpapers for inspiration and ideas.

The different thicknesses of yarn give interesting effects with 'patchwork knitting'. As only one or two double rows are knitted in any one yarn, for many of the designs you can easily combine shiny and matt yarns. Natural yarns are suitable but they should not be too thick.

ABBREVIATIONS

∨	Slip stitch
I	Knit
–	Purl
▲	Increase
2↑	Knit 2tog tbl
2↓	Knit 2tog
3↑	Knit 3 tog tbl
3↓	Knit 3tog
3←	Purl 3tog
KW	Knitwise
tbl	Through back of loop
M1	Make one stitch

Natural yarns can, for example, be very successfully combined with a thinner yarn which has a length of 180 m to 200 m per 50 g (needle size 3,5 mm).

The garments shown in this book are knitted with various types of yarns from different manufacturers (see suppliers, page 64). I have not given full details of the yarn and colours used as ranges are always changing and there are many beautiful yarns available. Let whatever you find inspire you to an exciting creation.

My tip:

Cut off and have ready pieces of yarn of about 1 m in length. This trick really forces you to change the colour as often as possible. Resulting in colourful and lively knitting.

The paper pattern

Before you pick up your needles, you need to have a paper pattern of the desired style. As most of the garments shown here tend to be based on rectangles or squares, this paper pattern has been made up accordingly. It can be easily adapted to an individual size by using your own pullover or jacket.

Every now and again, check the present state of your knitting against this paper pattern: simply place the pre-stretched knitting over it.

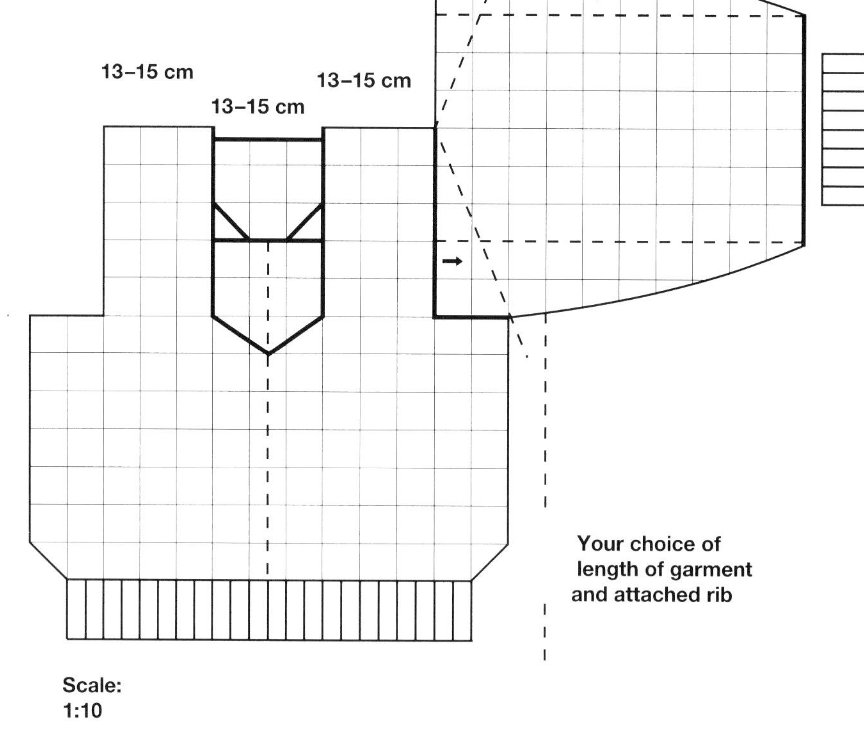

My tip:

Stretch out the pieces of knitting carefully. You can only determine the exact size and see the complete beauty of the knitting if you do this.

You can therefore easily see how many strips or pieces are needed to finish the work.

For the shaped parts of the sleeves you can either knit the shaped piece onto the finished square, or knit the whole piece right away using the pattern.

The straight edges of the shoulder pieces can be folded back from each side of the centre at a slight angle, and then sewn: usually a small shoulder pad is placed under the seam later.

Finally: the rib

In the 'old way of knitting' you always started with the rib. In 'patchwork knitting', the rib is knitted last. To prevent the rib losing its shape, it is advisable to knit it double.

It is best to start with a sleeve: this way you can easily see how many stitches produce how many centimetres of knitting. I usually use yarn with a length of about 100 m per 50 g ball of yarn. As a rule of thumb about 40–44

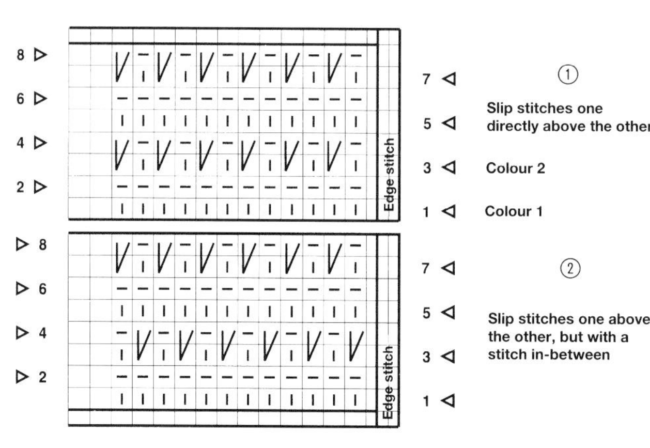

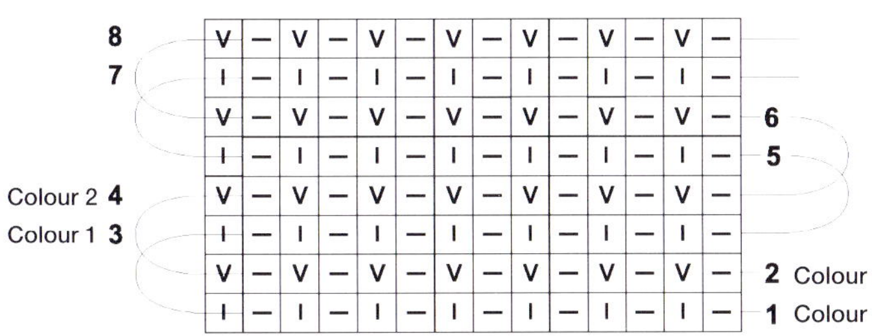

③

stitches are needed for a sleeve and about 80 stitches for each of the front and back pieces. For a rib, first knit all the edge stitches on the inside part of the piece onto a circular needle. In the second row decrease to the required number of stitches (by knitting two stitches together), or increase the stitches (make a stitch by picking up a horizontal loop before the next stitch and knitting into the back of it). Continue knitting stocking stitch until the desired length is reached, then knit one row purl for the fold line of the hem, now continue according to the rib pattern selected. Cast off the stitches very loosely (about 1 cm for every stitch) so that a row of purl is shown on the front side. Now simply fold back the rib and sew each stitch loosely on the reverse side. The cast-off row of stitches and the fold line should stretch as much as the knitted rib does.

Slip stitches make the rib especially firm. To achieve this, knit to the hem as described above, then continue knitting according to the illustration. It is best to use needles half a size bigger because you often only knit every other stitch (fig 1 & 2). It also looks good if you use a somewhat thicker yarn for the second colour. The rib can also be knitted in several different colours: in this case do not knit the inside rows in stocking stitch but start immediately with the pattern, for example purl 2, knit 2 (pay attention to the number of stitches). After you have finished knitting the row in the first colour do not turn it over. Start from the beginning again with the second colour (fig 3). Use needles with points at both ends or circular needles.

The yarn for the first colour can also be somewhat thicker. To get a neat finish, the number of stitches for the rib must be divisible by four, with two additional stitches left over. You get a good effect for the join if you start and finish the row with two purl stitches.

It is easier to knit the long rib for the jacket by working in three parts: the front borders and the neck. Then it is quite easy to check – and if necessary to correct – whether the right number of stitches has been knitted and if the dimensions are in order. Finally sew the three separate parts together neatly.

Style gallery

Strip jacket for men

For this attractive jacket, just follow the basic principles of 'patchwork knitting': strips, strips, and more strips.

First make a paper pattern in your actual size using strong brown paper. For this purpose it is best to take the measurements from an existing jacket that fits you comfortably.

For the first strip cast on 9 stitches.

Knit first two rows in stocking stitch in colour of your choice. Knit next 8 rows in garter stitch changing colour every two rows. Now knit next 12 rows in stocking stitch in one colour. Repeat the pattern as now set. Check the length of the strip with the paper pattern. Begin with the positioning of the pieces on the left side of the paper pattern.

When the strip has been cast off, use a circular needle to knit up the edge stitches from the right side. These stitches are joined to the second strip by the knitting method.

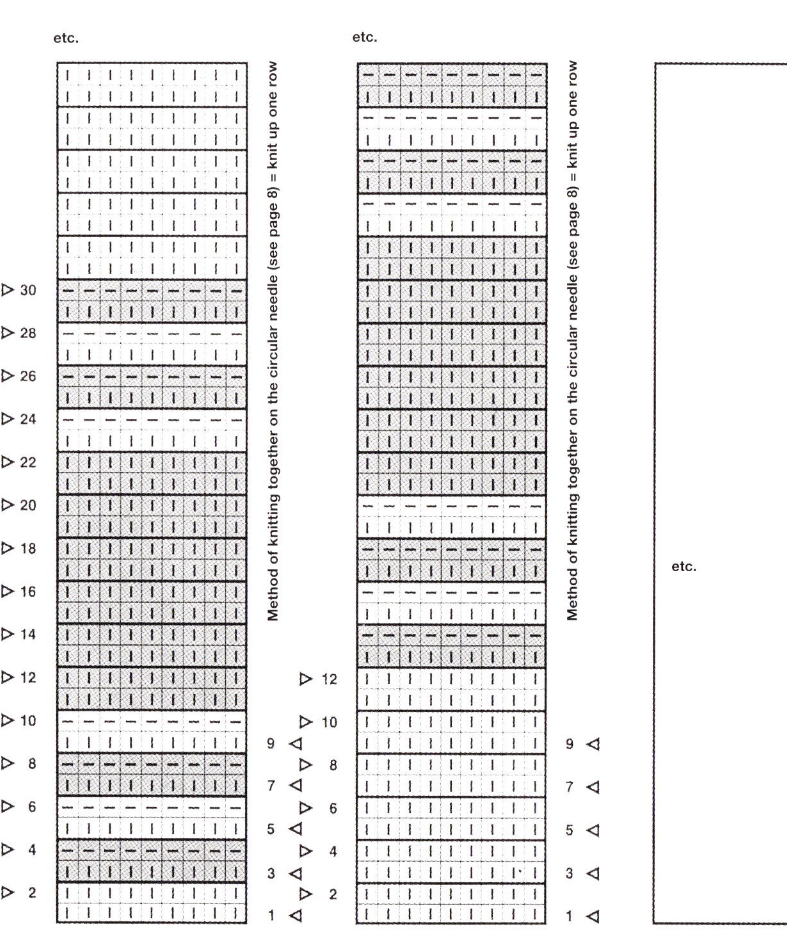

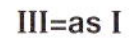

The pattern in the second strip begins with 12 rows of stocking stitch. To complete the jacket, knit the rib as described on pages 12 & 13. Do not forget the buttonholes on the front border.

You can make the jacket more versatile by not sewing on the sleeves, but rather attach them to the front and back piece with a zip (see photograph). In this way the jacket can be worn as a sleeveless waistcoat. The zip is hidden under a strip of trimming over the armhole knitted in garter stitch.

This is what the beginning of a strip for the man's jacket looks like. The actual pattern is produced by joining up the knitted strips.

Cable pattern for ladies

This pattern knitted in strips is certainly not an old-fashioned one. The bright shades of colour in the connecting rows give the garment added flair.

You saw the cable pattern pullover in striking red tones on pages 14 and 15, knit this design in strips as for the man's jacket. Cast on between 12 and 18 stitches for the first cable strip.

Three purl stitches are worked on each side of the cable. Choose your own type of cable for the stocking stitches in the middle.

Be daring in your choice of colours and cables: strips with different types of cable make the pullover an attractive eye-catcher.

Before knitting on the next strip, add another 4 rows using a decorative yarn on a circular needle. Then knit the strips together in the normal way.

I

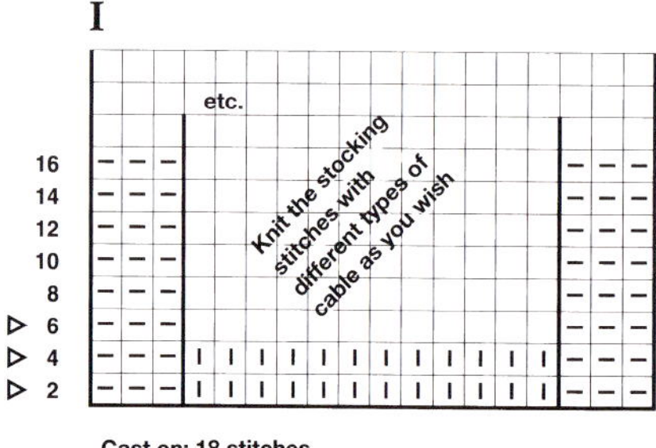

Cast on: 18 stitches

II

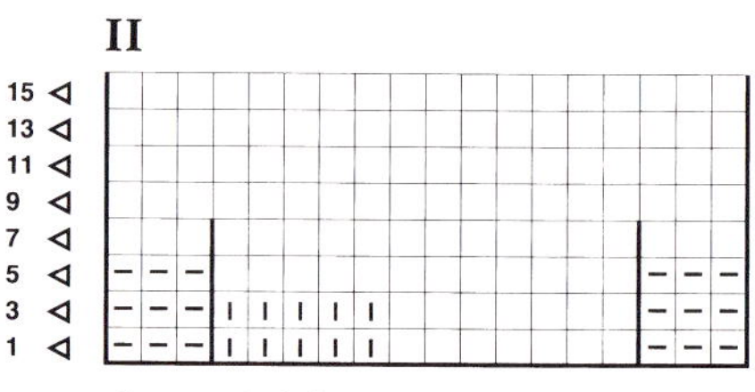

Cast on: 18 stitches

Soft tones in wool

This chic jacket in beige and pastel colours is knitted as for the man's jacket on pages 16 and 17. The wider strips make the soft tones appear nice and flat. In addition, attractive colour contrasts are achieved by knitting connecting rows in distinctive colours.

Diamond variations

Attractive patterns are produced by these long diamond strips. A striking design is also produced by the darker rows in garter stitch.

The diamond pattern made up of rectangular strips is produced by a clever colour change: begin with the darker contrast colour (17 stitches). This colour then runs through the whole strip. After a double row of garter stitch, knit in the other two colours in stocking stitch.

When the colours are changed, the

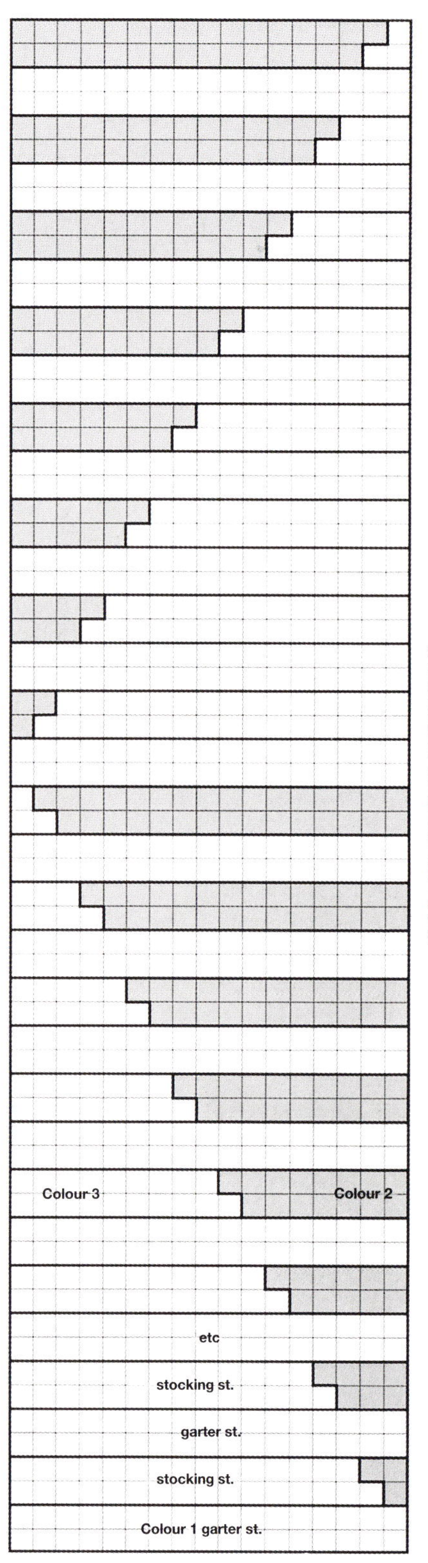

17 stitches

Knit the strips together in purl (see page 8)

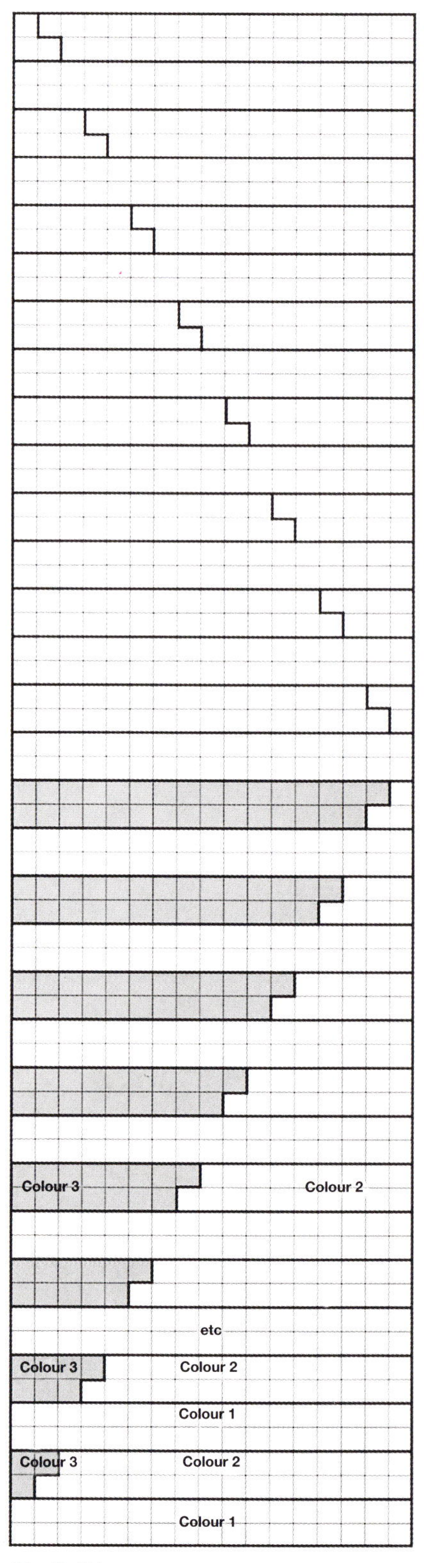

17 or 15 stitches

yarns are crossed over. It is advisable to cut the yarn of the two lighter colours of the diamonds to the appropriate lengths beforehand. In this way you prevent the yarns from becoming tangled unnecessarily. As the size of each coloured piece is exactly the same you can measure the correct length from the first piece.

When changing the yarns at the side you should make sure that the next colour is always taken up behind the first one, otherwise the joins will not look neat when the pieces are knitted together.

Knit the rectangular diamond strips together to finish the pullover as described on page 8.

Striking diamonds

Strips do not have to be rectangular: diamonds knitted point to point produce the structure of the knitting at a later stage.

As the strips of these diamonds are long you do not have to change the colours within the row. The pattern is the same as that of the rectangular diamonds: continuous dark rows knitted in garter stitch alternate between coloured double rows of stocking stitch.

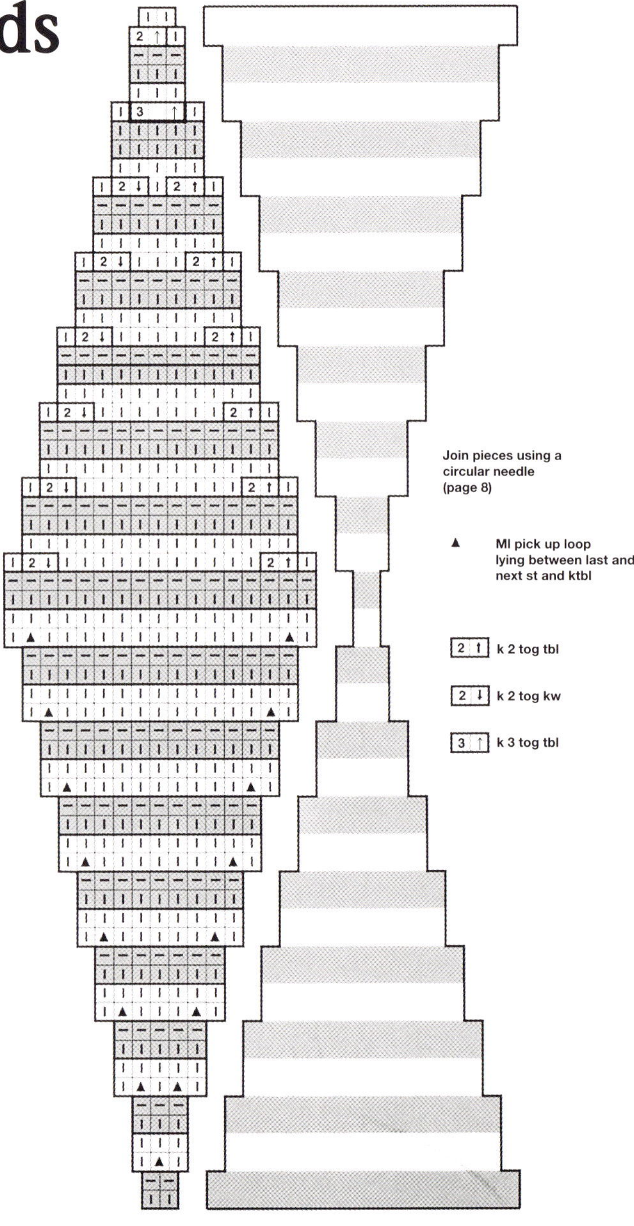

For this pattern simply increase the stitches in the positions marked on the chart in the lighter colour. To increase: Make a stitch by picking up a horizontal loop between the last and next stitch and knitting into the back of it.

When the piece has 17 stitches, begin casting off again after the dark row: at the edge decrease by knitting two stitches together following the chart abbreviations.

Continue following chart until diamond is complete.

Begin the second diamond with the middle row = 17 stitches (beginning of 2nd chart): carry on reducing stitches after the dark row of garter stitch. The diamond strips are then easily knitted together with a circular needle.

Now we go round

The strips of this pullover look rather like an hour-glass: the pattern with its colourful contrasts gives a soft and smooth effect.

As for the diamond strips on page 20, smart accents are also given to this design by its darker rows. The circles of the design are joined by rectangular insets so that they fit well together.

etc.

In the darker colour or in the colour that is to be used for knitting together.

In the darker colour or in the colour that is to be used for knitting together.

Stocking stitch

The strips fit together snugly due to the middle pieces, which are knitted straight

For the first strip begin with the rectangular piece in stocking stitch. Then increase the stitches for each row of the circle. When you have increased to 21 stitches knit four double rows in the corresponding colours before starting to decrease again.

Begin the second strip corresponding to the wide part of the circle so that the pieces can be joined together. As a connecting piece between the circle strips, knit a double row between the pieces in garter stitch on a circular needle using the method already shown (see pic above).

The square method

Squares are the main feature of this idea: besides working in strips you can also work in even smaller pieces and then knit them together as in patchwork. The square with diagonally decreasing stitches produces surprising patterns – and in addition leaves a lot of scope for your own creativity.

Again begin with an individual square. The next square is knitted from one side of the latter: thus knit half of the stitches from the existing side, and cast on the other half of the stitches.
In this way strips are formed again. You can also place the squares on end: when joined together a kind of patchwork technique is produced instead of the usual strips. However, cast off each individual square in the return row only!

Do not worry: the completed knitted piece becomes square when you cast off, even though it looks pyramid-shaped in the diagram.

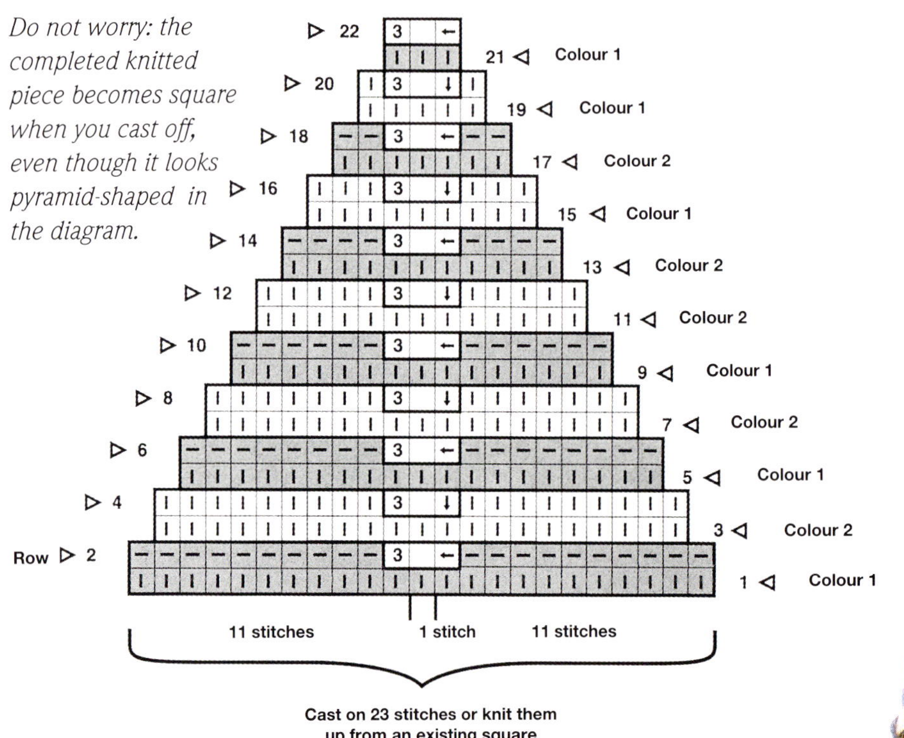

Each piece is an individual patch. Strips or angles can be formed when joining several of these pieces.

These squares form diamonds

Red and blue shades give real flair to this sporty jacket. The patches for this jacket are almost diamond-shaped, and each point has a small square in different shades of blue.

Cast on a total of 27 stitches for the first patch: 13 per side and one stitch extra. Always knit three stitches together in the middle of the return row. For the red and blue parts in moss stitch, the stitches should be knitted together as necessary. Continue knitting as many diamonds as needed for the width of the pullover.

The stitches for the second row of diamonds are then knitted up from the side edge stitches of the finished pieces (see diagram on page 29).

Do not forget to knit an additional middle stitch.

To summarise: knit up 13 stitches from the side edge stitches of the finished piece, cast on one more stitch for the middle, and then knit up 13 more stitches from the next finished piece. Continue knitting the next patch starting with these 27 stitches.

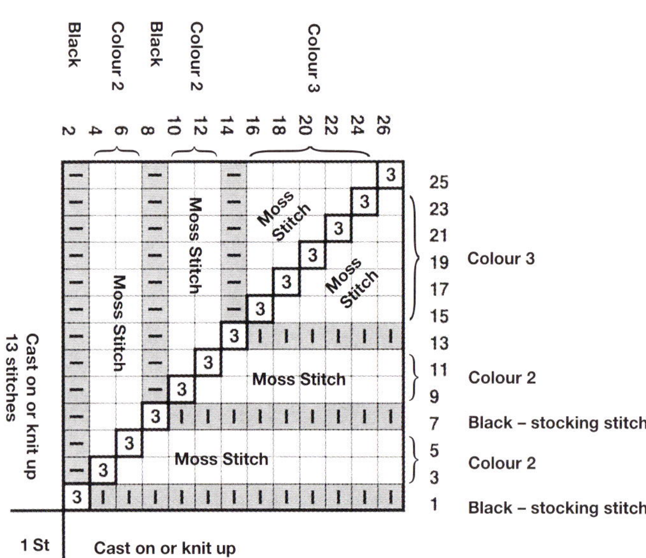

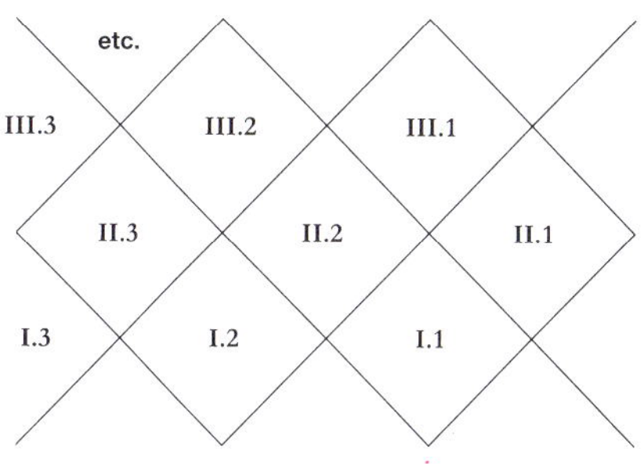

The sequence of the individual patches can be seen from the above drawing. I.1 is followed by II.1; then by III.1. Now continue with I.2 etc.

If only half a square is required as a filler – for example at the upper or lower edge of the knitting – you will only need to knit half a square... just knit two stitches together instead of three stitches.

Another triangle is produced if you cast off a stitch on the left and right side of the front. This does not affect the casting off on the reverse side.

Fleecy squares

This attractive lady's jacket is knitted in soft kid-mohair. The knitting method corresponds to the blue-red variation on page 28. The many shades of colours in fresh pastel tones make this garment look particularly smart.

Waistcoat in squares

The striking colours in this waistcoat are a colourful blue-green. The individual squares can of course be joined together into strips. The sporty waistcoat looks good with a plain shirt.

You can wear this smart eye-catcher at work or at leisure.

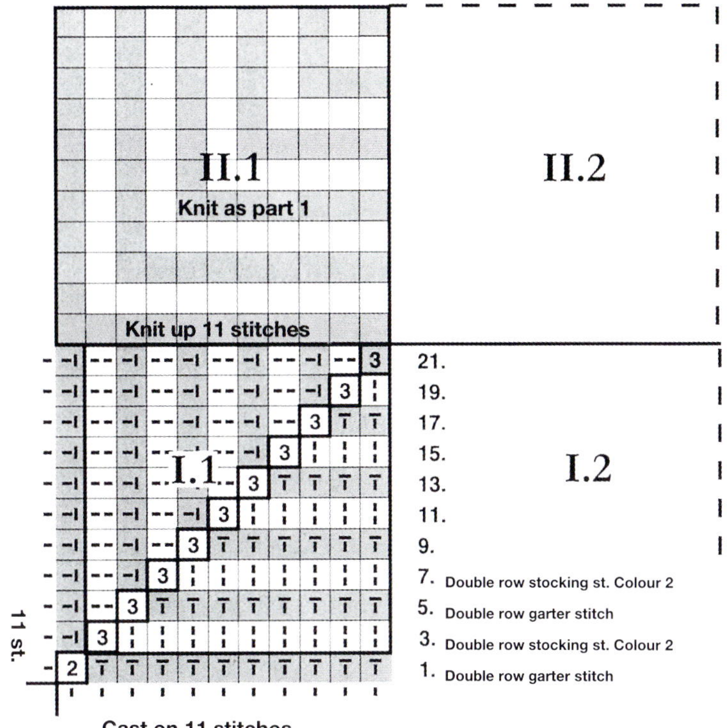

L-shaped patches

Instead of a complete square, L-shaped patches can also create an attractive pattern.

For this design, cast on 37 stitches as for a square (length of one side is 18 stitches). Cast on an extra 9 stitches for the longer side of the L-shape. Start knitting as for a square, but with unequal side lengths. Do not cast off in the middle, but after 27 stitches in the return row. When you still have 10 stitches plus middle stitch plus 20 stitches cast off 10 stitches on the return row. Knit the remaining 10 stitches according to method 3 with the longer side of the "L", so that a smaller square is produced. Cast off again on the reverse side. Here the middle square is knitted in garter stitch with thin kid-mohair yarn.

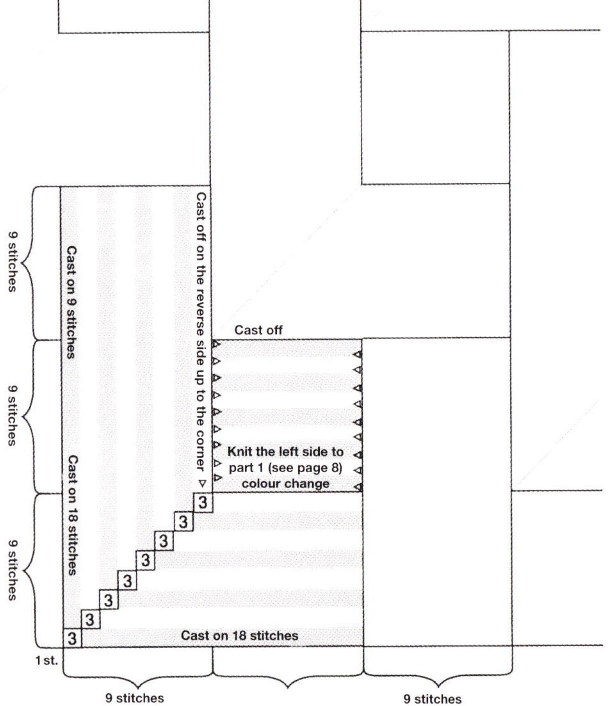

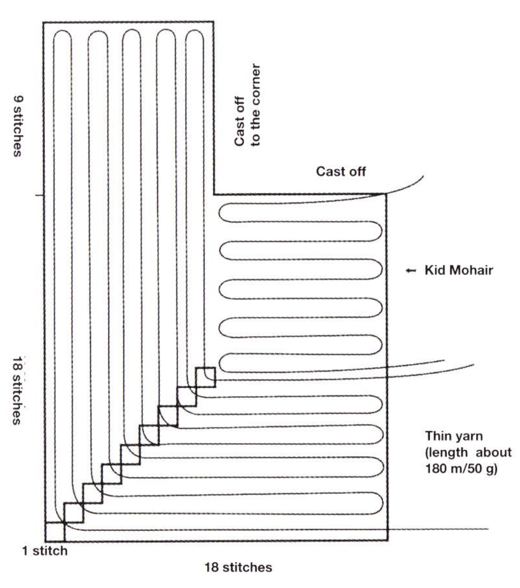

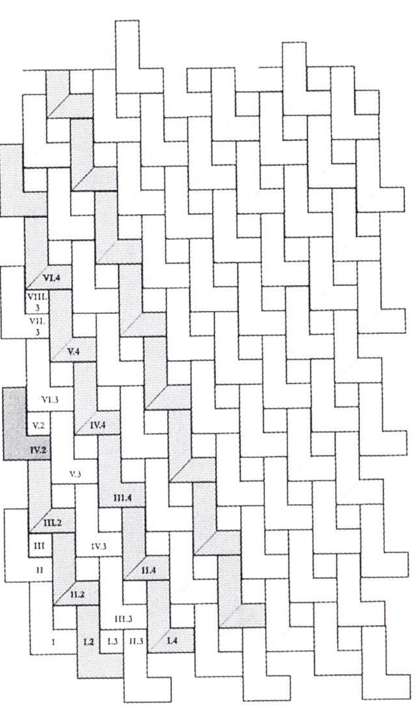

Begin knitting with Part I, then continue with parts II and III etc. After these, follow with parts I.2, II.2, III.2 etc. Knit the angled pieces according to the sequence in the diagram.

Two completely different jackets – and yet both are knitted according to the 'square' method. The man's jacket is described in detail on page 56.

Multi-coloured jacket

This jacket is certainly not incomplete even though the squares – two adjoining squares in each case – appear as half squares

The appearance of the squares overlapping each other is produced by the darker contrast yarn bordering the bottom edge; and omitted at the top edge. Thus the squares look as if they are open at the top.

The rows where the stitches are decreased produce a decorative diamond lattice. For this jacket, always knit two squares at a time. It will save both time and work!

Patchwork in colour

Bright shades in strong colours are used for this jacket. The pattern consists of two squares knitted together, one a normal square, the other a latticed rectangle. However, contrary to the previous design, this jacket is knitted from top to bottom; begin at the shoulders and knit down to the rib.

'T' squares

This idea was inspired by the letter 'T'. With small connecting square pieces between them, the T-shapes can be placed in a staggered arrangement.

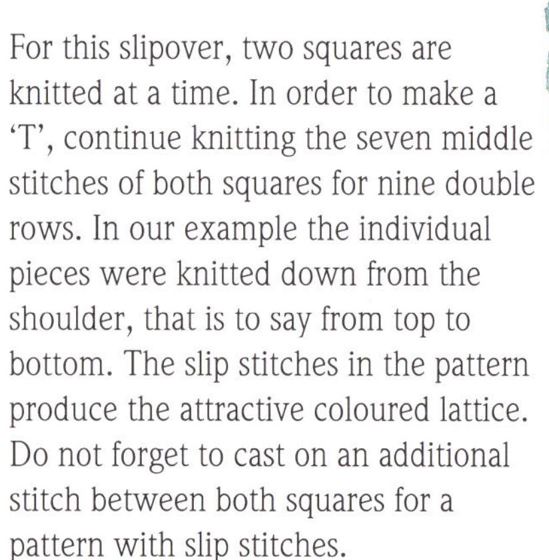

For this slipover, two squares are knitted at a time. In order to make a 'T', continue knitting the seven middle stitches of both squares for nine double rows. In our example the individual pieces were knitted down from the shoulder, that is to say from top to bottom. The slip stitches in the pattern produce the attractive coloured lattice. Do not forget to cast on an additional stitch between both squares for a pattern with slip stitches.

A round affair

The short-waisted pullover is knitted completely out of 'round' patches. For this design always knit two squares at a time. To make pieces round, cast off stitches at random, not only in the middle. But it is important that you decrease stitches only on the return row.

Turn about squares

This attractive design in a lightly mottled, coloured yarn is easier to knit than appears at first sight. Instead of knitting just one square at a time, knit three squares. This saves time and is really not so complicated. From a square that is three-quarters finished, knit up the stitches for the next square and cast on the additional stitches required. Individual squares fill up the pullover. In our design the mottled grey rows are knitted in garter stitch and the coloured rows are knitted in stocking stitch

Here three squares are knitted at a time. The structure is produced by alternative rows knitted in garter stitch with a mottled yarn, and rows knitted in stocking stitch with a solid coloured yarn.

Colours behind bars

Squares look completely different when you use slip stitches, colours peep out at intervals, as if from behind a lattice.

Again, as in the preceding design, three squares are knitted at a time. The arrangement of the pieces is also the same. But instead of knitting plain or purl, knit with slip stitches: thus in every second double row, work one stitch and slip one stitch (see chart).

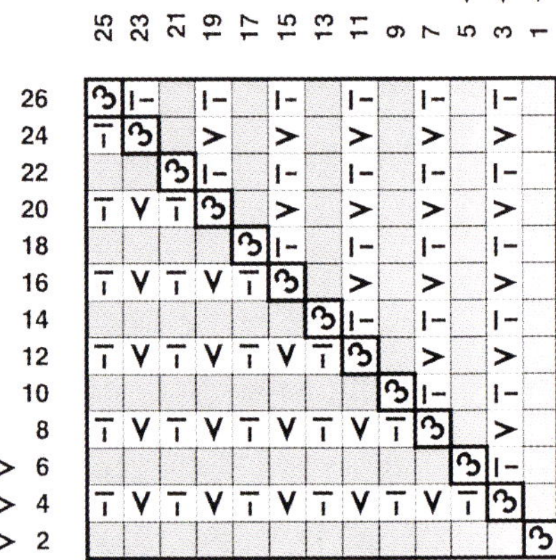

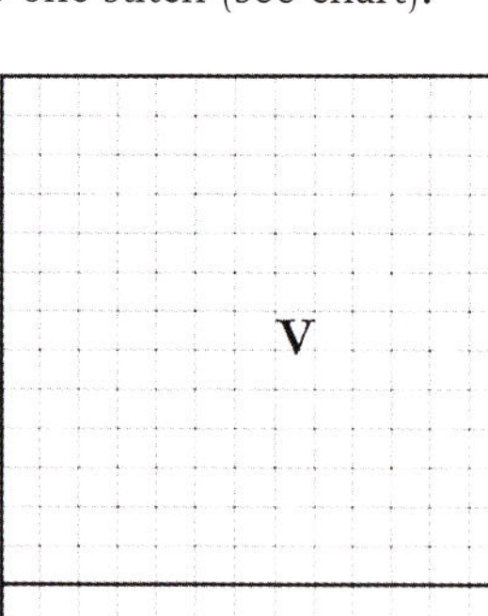

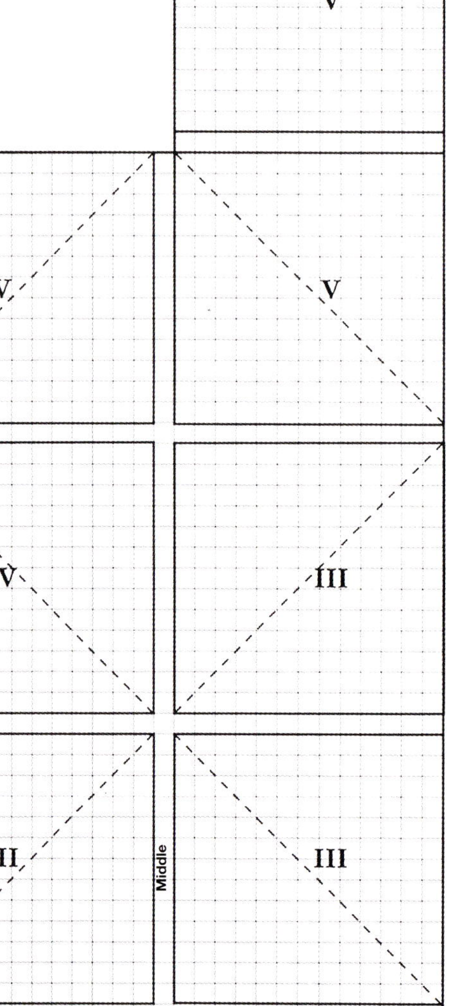

Knitting three squares at a time is no problem even with slip stitches. You only need to cast on one extra stitch between the basic patterns of the individual squares. So you always have one stitch more between two squares.

Black and grey jacket

This jacket is a smart and unusual piece of knitting because of the variety of patterns and yarns used. The knitting method is exactly the same as for the pullover on page 40. However, many different types of knitting are involved in this jacket. Instead of just plain rows, rows of stocking and garter stitch alternate with rows of moss stitch. Individual pieces knitted with mohair provide further interesting accents

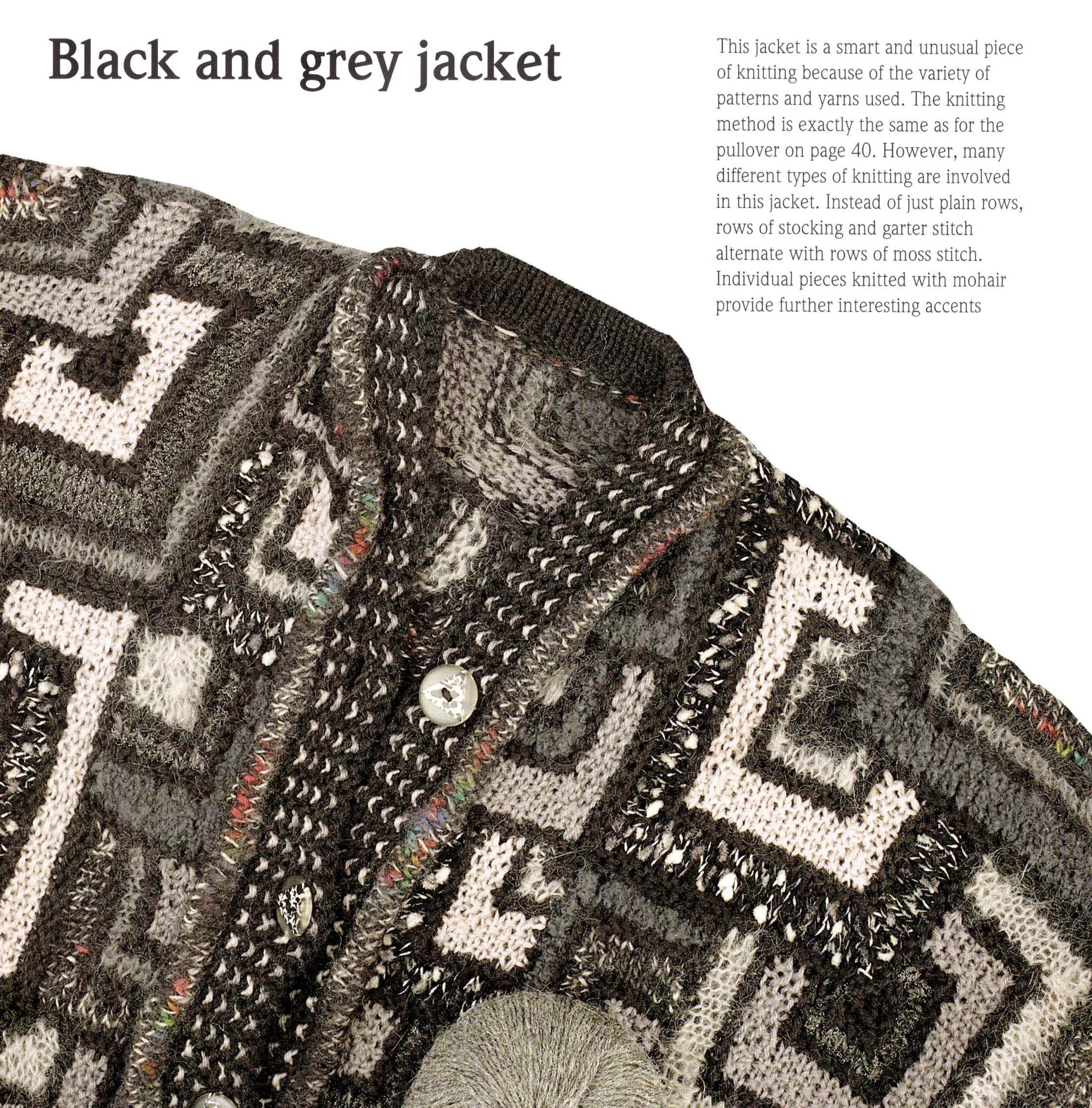

Pink fantasy

'Round' patches and different yarns are the distinguishing features of this piece of knitting. Knit the individual pieces with different types of yarn: long-haired mohair, shiny decorative yarn, mixtures of wool and acrylic. Arrange the different pieces as you prefer.

Just mix circles from one, two or three squares. The dark rows that begin each 'round' patch produce attractive contrasts. The circles are formed by casting off in different places in the return row, so do not always knit the two middle stitches together.

Chic in zig-zag

This jacket with its strong colours is an example of how creative you can be in arranging the squares. This time the individual staggered pieces are not completed with a triangle at the bottom, Therefore a zig-zag edge is produced as a result. The bright colours and the swinging tassels make this an attention-grabbing jacket. Begin the short jacket at the top, knit long strips and finish off underneath with squares that are knitted (or sewn) together in the middle with two knitting needles.

Baroque stitches

Blue, green and gold are the colours of this stylish pullover. Shiny glass stones give additional accents. The gold accent yarn which produces a glittery appearance is worked into several squares. Here too the individual pieces are knitted round in order to reinforce the decorative character of the pattern.

Circles, circles, circles

Circles with dark connecting insets produce an attractive pattern. Black is the basic colour here. The slip stitches are knitted in shades of red and violet.

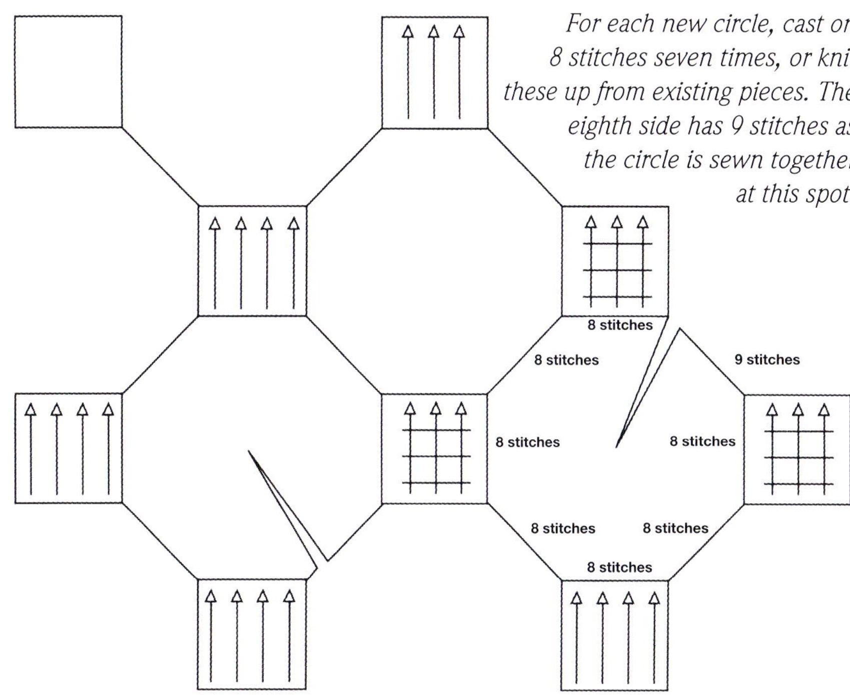

For each new circle, cast on 8 stitches seven times, or knit these up from existing pieces. The eighth side has 9 stitches as the circle is sewn together at this spot.

First begin with all the black insets. To knit these squares cast on 9 stitches and knit 9 double rows alternating with garter stitch and slip stitch. Finally cast off on the reverse side.

To complete a knitted circle you will need 65 stitches. Cast on 8 stitches in the coloured wool and then knit 8 stitches from an existing square (8 x 8 + 1 stitch, see diagram). Knit the next two double rows in moss stitch. The black yarn is used in the third double row, and this is knitted in slip stitch (1 stocking stitch, 1 slip stitch). Now knit another coloured double row in moss stitch, knitting 2 stitches together in the return row. Follow this method until the third double row in slip stitch, then knit a double row in moss stitch and cast off. Neatly sew together the joins of the still open circle.

You can either sew together the individual circles and cubes, or join them while you are knitting.

Arrange the 'bricks' as if building a wall

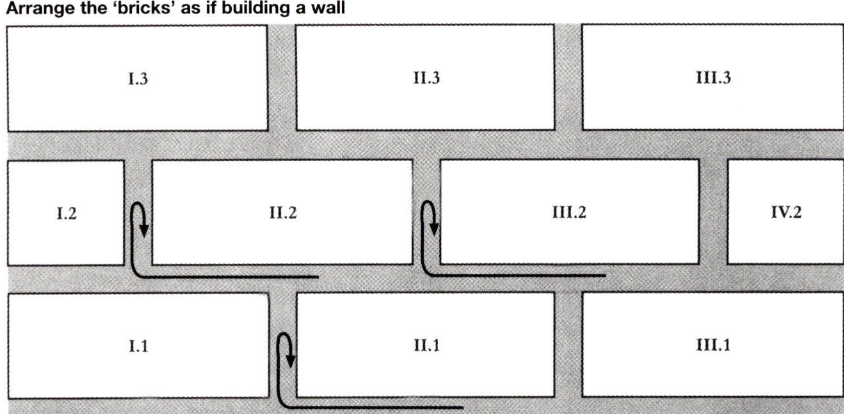

Brick and mortar are knitted together according to method 3

Brick pattern

This extraordinary jacket has a pattern copied from a brick wall. Piece for piece this design is composed of 19 different shades of red. A light mottled yarn holds the individual pieces together as the 'mortar'.

Begin knitting as for a rectangle with unequal sides. Cast on 18 plus 7 stitches in the light 'mortar' colour. Knit two rows stocking stitch, casting off one stitch in the corner. Then in moss stitch knit the 17 stitches of the longer side in a red shade. Bricks and mortar are knitted together with the circular needle method. After a total of 14 rows, cast off on the reverse side in knit so that the purl side appears on the right side.

The rows of bricks are simply knitted off-centre from each other in the same way as bricks are arranged on a real wall.

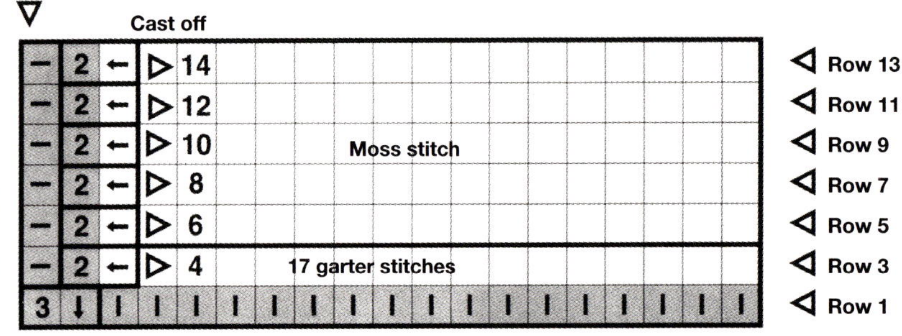

Circles and nets

With this garment you can give your imagination free rein: the jacket in 'round' and 'square' patches lends itself to the expression of creativity. Again, knit three 'squares' at the same time for these circles.

Cast off at random in moss stitch so that circles are produced instead of squares. The netlike structure of the small squares which are knitted beforehand is produced by slip stitches: after each coloured double row knit a double row in slip stitch. A white yarn makes a good 'background' colour for the small squares.

Palette of denim blue

The colours of this comfortable pullover with a buttoned neck detail are arranged like a staircase. Rows of different coloured yarns are used in between the different shades of blue of the individual squares to give a warm and interesting effect.

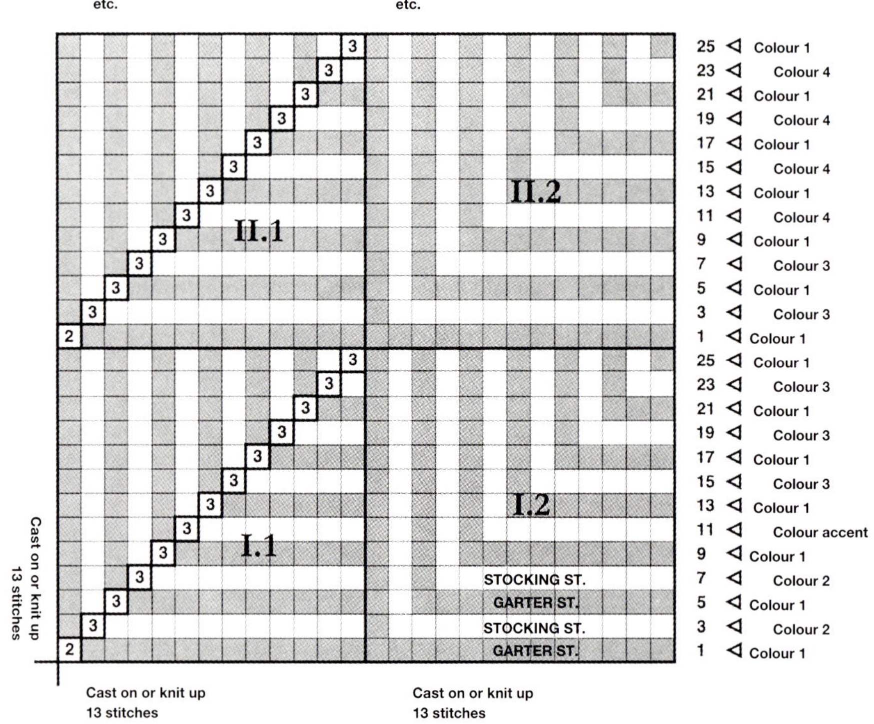

The attractive pattern of this pullover is achieved by a clever change of colour: simply begin each square with the blue shade and the colour which was used in the preceding square. For each square, cast on 27 stitches. Cast off as usual in the middle of the return row. Knit alternate rows of stocking and garter stitch in blue. In the eleventh row, knit in a contrasting colour in red, yellow or green.

In order to produce a mirror-like image of the pattern you have to work on two sides: lay the first half of the front piece on the left side of your pattern. The second half is then produced working from the right. Strips worked in the colours of the rib are used to join the pieces of the pullover: in our model four rows of purl in a mottled yarn are used, then three double rows of slip stitches are knitted in two different colours. Finish off with 4 rows of purl again using a mottled yarn.

These separating strips are knitted on the back, front, sides and sleeves.

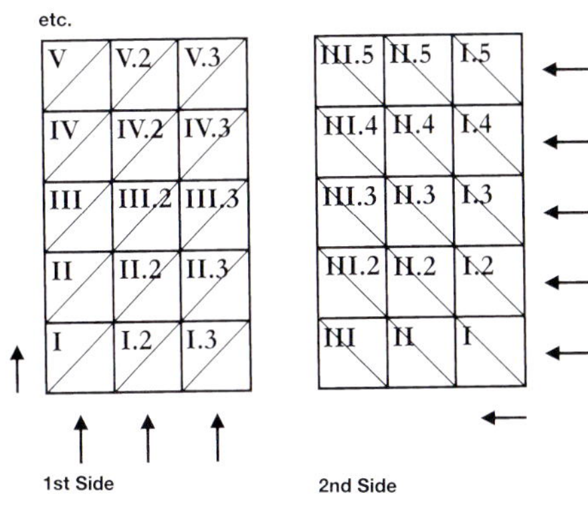

cables – down and across

You can knit this design in shades of brown or in strong colours: whatever you choose the cable pattern makes the pullover something special and unique.

Cast on 22 stitches for the cable pieces: the darker colour in the first row creates a contrast. Knit two cable patches next to each other as illustrated in the diagram. Knit 22 double rows for each piece. End each piece with a row of the darker colour.

For the next cable piece cast on 22 stitches at the left upper edge of the first piece. The second piece is knitted together with the first one on the reverse side as follows: slip the last stitch knitwise, knit an edge stitch from the needle and pass the slipped stitch over it. You can also knit the last edge stitch and the stitch from the needle together into the back of the stitch. This is quicker, and has the same result.

This pattern has two adjoining cable pieces. The second piece is placed horizontally.

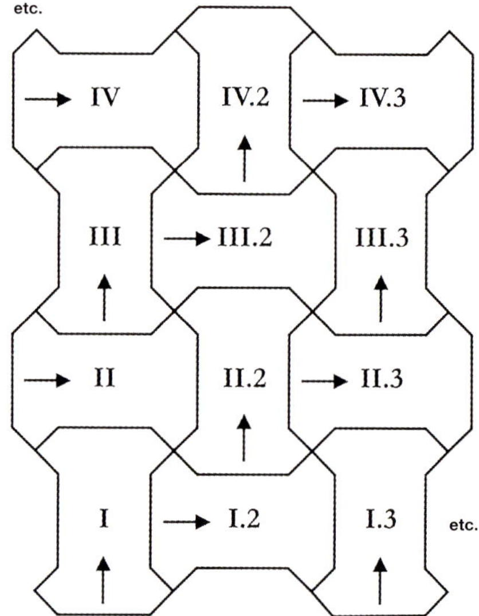

Knit the individual pieces as shown in the diagram and join them together in the sequence indicated: Part I is followed by parts II, III, and IV, then by parts I.2, II.2, III.2 and IV.2.

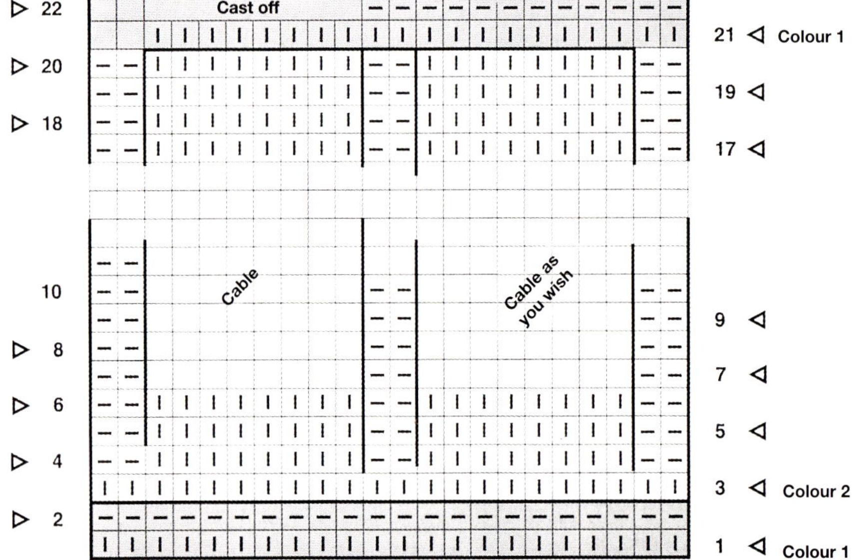

Cube effects

A popular patchwork pattern is the idea behind the designs on these pages. The colours are arranged in such a way that the knitted cubes appear three-dimensional.

The block pattern is as effective in yellow and brown shades, as the sportier waistcoat in red and blue using a finer yarn. (Page 58).

Strictly speaking, the cube shape for this pattern is knitted in two parts: the sides and the 'lid'. Cast on 23 stitches for both of the front pieces. In the front row only two stitches are added. The casting off is done on the reverse row. The principle is the same as for the squares – but this time the decreased stitches are increased again at the edges. With this technique the number of stitches remains the same, and a kind of 'V' is produced.

For the upper square of the cube continue knitting with the stitches from the right half of the piece.

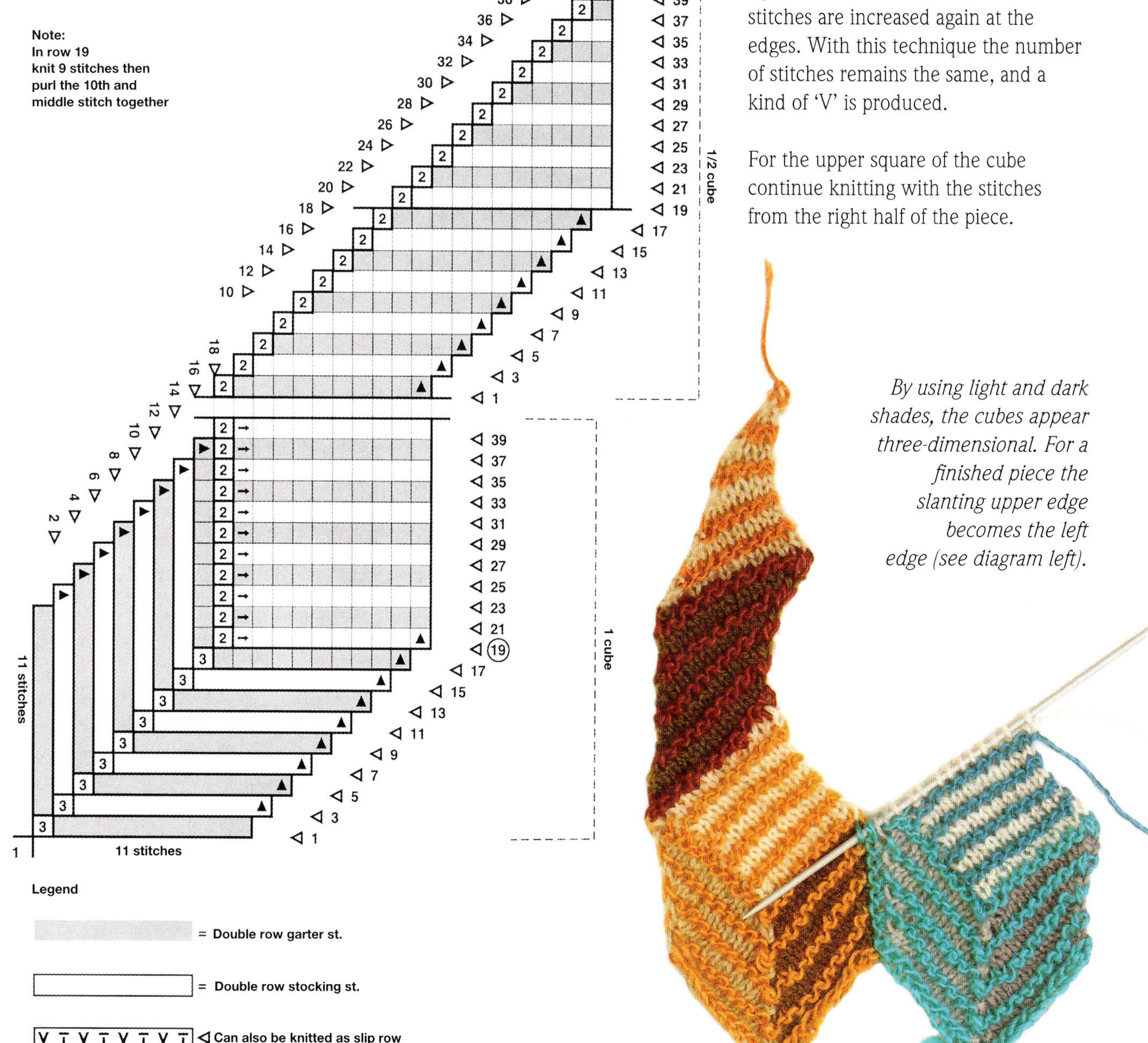

By using light and dark shades, the cubes appear three-dimensional. For a finished piece the slanting upper edge becomes the left edge (see diagram left).

Just knit without increasing or decreasing. The square is knitted together purlwise on the left side with the finished piece.

The sequence of the individual pieces is based on traditional patchwork. Place the first block on the bottom left of the paper pattern, the second piece is joined to the left side above it. Then begin again at the bottom, to the right side of the first block, placing the further parts running diagonally from right to left. In order to keep a straight edge many of the blocks are only half squares.

Within each cube the colours are distributed so that the lighter colours are on top, and the darker colours on the right. This produces a three-dimensional effect when the knitting is finished. When crossing colours within a row, knit the middle stitch with both colours. The pattern is the same for all three sides of the cube: one double row stocking stitch, one double row garter stitch. Alternating colours after each double row also makes the garment particularly attractive.

Cubes in Turquoise

This waistcoat can be worn on any occasion. The clever cube pattern and turquoise lattice will brighten any outfit.

The blocks of this design are similar to those of the jacket and waistcoat on pages 56 to 58. However, instead of knitting in rows of stocking and garter stitch, these cubes are knitted with slip stitches. Just knit every second stitch in a coloured yarn and slip the stitches of the turquoise yarn along the row. This produces a lattice pattern that runs through the waistcoat uniformly.

Jacket with shells

The patchwork principle also works with shapes other than squares: the knitted shell looks rather complicated, but is not as difficult to knit as it seems.

Always begin each shell at the wide end. For this reason the jacket is best knitted downwards from the shoulders. For the first shell, cast on 33 stitches and knit the return row in stocking stitch. Then knit a double row in garter stitch.

Using this method you can produce the pointed shells to make the jacket on page 61.

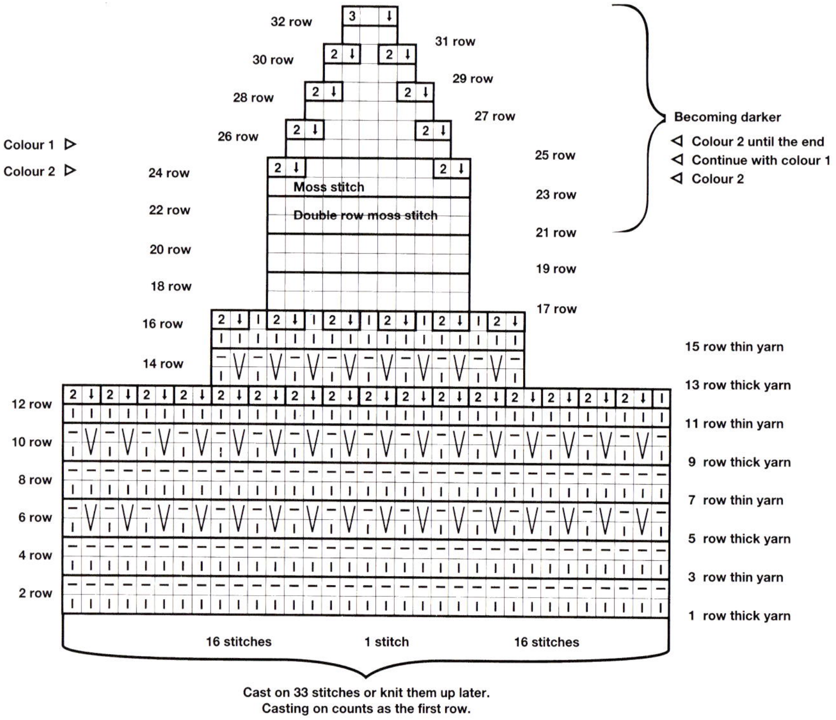

Colour 1 ▷
Colour 2 ▷

32 row, 31 row, 30 row, 29 row, 28 row, 27 row, 26 row, 25 row, 24 row, 23 row, 22 row, 21 row, 20 row, 19 row, 18 row, 17 row, 16 row, 14 row, 12 row, 10 row, 8 row, 6 row, 4 row, 2 row

Moss stitch
Double row moss stitch

Becoming darker
◁ Colour 2 until the end
◁ Continue with colour 1
◁ Colour 2

15 row thin yarn
13 row thick yarn
11 row thin yarn
9 row thick yarn
7 row thin yarn
5 row thick yarn
3 row thin yarn
1 row thick yarn

16 stitches | 1 stitch | 16 stitches

Cast on 33 stitches or knit them up later.
Casting on counts as the first row.

If you knit the middle part of the shells up to the 32nd row without decreasing stitches, and then cast off, you will produce shells with a flat end (see the diagrams above left, below, and below right).

The second double row is also knitted in garter stitch, but in a different colour and with a thinner yarn. Knit the third double row with slip stitches: knit one stitch, slip one. Knit five alternate double rows. In the return row of the sixth double row knit two stitches together. After a further double row in slip stitch, knit two stitches together in the return row, then make one stitch by knitting into front and back of the stitch, so that there are still 17 stitches on the needle. Then knit three double rows with a thinner yarn, in the next four return rows one stitch is cast off at both ends (= two per row). Knit the last three stitches together.

Start knitting the shell jacket at the shoulders. You can produce effective results by skillfully distributing the colours.

List of suppliers

Most types of yarn are suitable for the technique developed by Horst Schulz. The models shown in the book were, for the most part, made with yarns from the firms *Online, Rowan, and Zürcher & Co. Online* and *Zürcher & Co* will gladly give you information about outlets near you where the desired yarns can be obtained.

Online
Klaus Koch Gmbh & Co. KG
Rheinstrasse
35260 Stadtallendorf
Germany

Rowan
Distributors for Germany:
Wolle und Design
Rosmarie Kaufmann
Wolfshovener Strasse 76
52428 Jülich-Setternich
Germany

Saprotex International (Pty) Ltd.
P.O. Box 1293
East London
5200
Phone: +27 043 7631531
Fax: +27 043 7631929

You can order complete wool packages for Schulz models from the following address:

Franz Schlosser
Albert-Schweitzer-Strasse 1
38226 Salzgitter
Germany

Acknowledgements

My grateful thanks go to the following people who contributed towards making this book a reality:
Henk and Henriette Beukers, who were the first people to recognise the novelty of my technique and who often published my patterns in the magazine "Ornamente", Franz Schlosser, who arranged invitations to fairs through the firm *Online* and so introduced me to the professional world.
My lady and gentlemen pupils who successfully used my idea of 'patchwork knitting' in their work.
All those knitters in distant countries who turned my ideas into beautiful garments by means of my explanations by letter, despite our different languages.
To the knitters whose garments feature in this book: Christa Bucker, Karola Mahlkow, Helga Müller, Wilhelma Naujok, Phylis Nixon and Anette Raschke.
My former pupils who arranged workshops on their own to teach the techniques of my 'patchwork knitting'.
My friend Norman Fisher who produced the manuscript with endless patience, often from illegible and incoherent text.
Sylvia Hank who prepared the manuscript for printing.
Finally, to Augustus Verlag, who published this book.

I hope this book will help revive a beautiful, although rather neglected hobby, and also re-awaken the creativity in many people.

We all have talents – we only have to discover them.

Horst Schulz

Also published by Saprotex International by Horst Schulz:
New Knitting: Fashions for Children

The author and publisher thank the firm Breitschwerdt Holzspielzeug for the kind support for the photographs.

Photography: Annette Hempfling, Munich
Graphics/drawings: Manuela Junkte, Leipzig
Jacket design: Christa Manner, Munich
Layout: Walter Werbegrafik, Gundelfingen

Augusutus Verlag, Augsburg 1997

Published in English in 2000 by
Saprotex International (Pty) Ltd
PO Box 1293, East London, 5200, South Africa
Production & printing co-ordinator:
Unifoto International (Pty) Ltd
Printed in Singapore by Tien Wah Press Pte Ltd